Pathways *to* Love

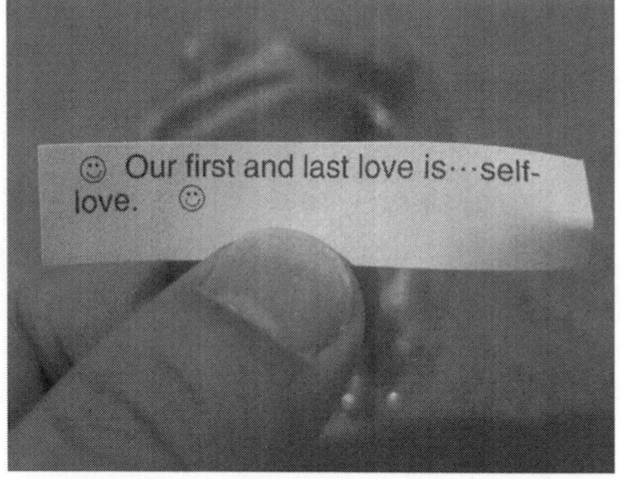

Pathways to Love

28 Days to Self LUove

SHAWN ROOP

Jai Media - San Diego, CA
2010

Published by Jai Media
San Diego, California

Library of Congress-in-Publication Data

Roop, Shawn

Pathways to Love: 28 Day to Self Love / Shawn Roop

ISBN: 1451570945
EAN-13: 9781451570946

Publishing Manger: Beth Elder
Content Readers: Beth Elder, Tracey Lontos, Derrick Koch
Cover Design and Layout: Shawn Roop
Editing and Proofreader: Judy Kamande, Krizelle Estorpe and Beth Elder
Author Photograph: Tracey Lontos
Typeset: Book Antiqua, New Times Roman, Garamond

Acknowledgments

My Teachers:
Dr. Corynna Clarke *who saw my calling before I did,* ***Osho*** *for sharing Mahamudra and life wisdom in a deep way,* ***Maha Chandra*** *who is no longer here but still teaches me,* ***Tilopa, Tad James*** *who woke my magic and spirit up,* ***Roger and Shirley Elliott (my parents)*** *who always loved and took care of me in my quest to live a life well lived.* ***Every Student*** *and* ***Client*** *I have had.*

My Peers:
Kamala Devi *for showing me new ways to live creatively,* ***Baba Dez*** *for being a true peer,* ***Ariel White*** *for playing while working,* ***Luna*** *for teaching me hard lessons in loving ways, and* ***Moses Ma*** *for seeing something in me even when I couldn't.*

Derrick Koch *for knowing me since 6th grade, becoming my best friend and always allowing me to grow.*

Richard Roop*, my brother, who helped me to learn NLP when I was 18 and showing me what success in self help looks like.*

My Love Tribe in San Diego:
Beth Elder, Tracey Lontos, Adam Paulman, Kamala Devi, Jude Mathis, Viraja Prema, Kypris Aster, Robin Church *and her runways,* ***Paul Anthony, Francoise Ginsberg,*** *and everyone in my* ***Tantra Theater troupe: Michael, Ember, Joy,*** *and* ***Rita:*** *The love from all of you in San Diego is amazing and pure.*

Larry Michael *for pushing me to get writing and share myself with the world. This book would not be without him.*

Dedication

*To **Beth**:*
You have seen me, celebrated me and supported me in ways no one has. Your love, encouragement and acceptance permit me to love myself more. Our relationship has helped me come home to my center. Thank you honey for allowing me to love myself, so I can love you so hugely!

*To **Myself**:*

Thanks for accepting all of my failure and success and still allowing love, greatness and grace to bathe my life. The journey I am on is so wonderful; challenging at times, but mostly a celebration of all that is in each breath the best way I know how. With kind eyes, full heart and deep acceptance, I love you.

Your Time...

"Start the journey, rather than figuring out the destination. The happiness is found not in finishing an activity but, truly, in being in the experience."

Shawn Roop

Table of Contents

Introduction

There are many ways to explore love. In this book, it's important to state that love looks, feels, tastes and sounds very different to each one of us. You know that, right?

This book is for those who understand, and want, love, but don't know how to put it into practice. We may have felt and shared love, but for some reason that hasn't been enough. Many people want *more* love, others want *new* love. Some want to know what love is and others just need love. (This is starting to sound like the very ideas that made every 80's love song!)

Over the years, I have supported thousands of people in exploring these questions. Mostly, they ask the big question, *"How do I find love?"* I smile and say, *"The real question is not 'how to', but rather, 'what is in the way'?"*

The block to what they want is not another person, past emotions or failed strategies. These lead and contribute to the issues; yet the core issue is **us**. It's not *outside of us*. If you can accept responsibility for your life and how you explore love, the victim state can be released. This is one of the most empowering things you can do...

Many people just don't know, or for that matter, like, themselves. You may have had years of looking outside to fulfill love's needs, which has created a sort of co-dependent behavior. It's how we were raised; and now the time has come to re-evaluate and see what really works for you, and what doesn't.

This is a 28 day experience; an opportunity to open up, know and love **YOU** better. This allows others to receive you in healthy and expansive ways.

Why 28 days? Well, it's 4 weeks, one trip around the moon. Within those 4 weeks, this will create trust, knowledge and understanding of how you tick. You will see your **passion** and your **roadblocks**. By knowing your design better, it offers a deeper mastery of how you experience love. You will uncover old stuff, discover new stuff and reclaim energy and emotions that may be the very thing that keeps your love from burning the way you want it to. Be gentle, open and available. This is not a test. This is about learning **HOW TO LOVE YOU**, which will give you a fantastic foundation in sharing love with everyone around you.

I have used these exercises to create a torrid *love affair with me.* It's been a rocky road at times, but I'm still committed. I keep finding new ways to know myself. It has offered me safety and security to open up my heart and love others without limitations. And this is the most liberating gift.

Let's talk about love…

The Love Story

"You, yourself, as much as anybody in the entire universe, deserve your love and affection."

Buddha

So many seek the comfort of things related to romance, to create models and strategies for what love "should" look like. Many desire a romantic love affair as learned from movies, fairytales and music. Even if they have never experienced nor witnessed anyone who has ever even had a romantic affair over the ages, they still search for it; dreaming of a later day where true love penetrates the soul and ends happily ever after, the goal being - to find that one to fit the bill. So, they continue to seek and look for this Holy Grail. It's this idea of the grand adventure and the things dreams are made of; the *"perfect love"*!

However, how many seek love with the one person that will be with them for the rest of their lives? How many are aware of the importance of such a relationship? How many get that that relationship is right here (at the right place), and right now (at the right time)? Yes, every person reading this is already in the most important love affair one could ever know.

It's within you.

You are in the most important relationship you could ever be in. How are you doing? How does it feel that I just put it out there? It kind of messes with the power of fairytale story lines, poems, Valentine's Day ideas and romance movies, doesn't it? All of that Disney-like romance, that leads to two people sharing life together forever as the grand finale of a successful measure of the heart... I mean if you grew up in the west, this society has not let you really know much more. Some of you may have been shielded, others disheartened and then some even end up rebelling against the whole thing.

The issue is that there are years of foundational beliefs that are at the very root of how we relate to loving.

Are you ready to rethink this model that has been forcefully fed into you?

Are you ready to start loving yourself first?

So many people say to me, *"Ah, Shawn, that's great and all, but I want someone to wake up with, to eat with! I've been with myself already!"*

Many people don't like the company or relationship with themselves. And if you are bored with yourself, why would anyone else want to be with you? If you don't completely love yourself, who would really love you? Would you want that? Maybe you have had it, and you know what I am talking about. This is about **loving you** the way you might love your soul mate.

You hold in your hand a series of practices that will take you to a new level of how you approach each day, how to open your heart and how to deeply know the most amazing person in your life—you!

This book has a system designed to offer you 28 days of practices and techniques to expand your love and you will no longer wait for your ultimate relationship to find you. The daily practices are designed to create:

- De-armoring
- Better knowing of your body
- Great connection to your heart
- Self-knowing
- Stress reduction
- Well being
- Playfulness
- Sex appeal
- Healthy selfishness
- Peaked awareness
- Heart-centered courage

The great news is that you are already in the most wonderful relationship that you can't get out of! You can deny it. You can fight it. You can even hate it. But even so, dear friends, I am here to share that you really already are in the right relationship; right here and right now! The choice is yours.

Learn yourself, and let your **self-love** become so abundant that you begin to attract amazing people to share that love with you. We have heard it before, *"When you're not looking for love, love finds you."* The reason is because one who actively *is* in love with themselves becomes an amazing *magnet* to others.

This book will help you regain joy in loving yourself…

How This Book Works

There are 28 days of practices in finding a better relationship with you in this book. These are all for you. There are no rules as to how you should approach the order of each practice. I have some suggestions on how you can use this book, however, if you like something, do it again. Let it be an add-on to your new day's practice. I strongly feel that it's powerful to keep doing new things in the cycle, but if you do get results that you consider good, keep using it.

Your intention is not just to do the day's exercises, but rather, really finding the juice of these gems and how much they break the day-to-day pattern you may have created for yourself. **The more you break the cycle, the more you create choice to enjoy change.** There are no goals to reach, but rather a deep awareness and exploration of the love affair you have with yourself.

Look, you are the one who is taking this path to self love. There's more to it than just doing a few of the 28 days and saying, *"I have self love!"* That's great! However, there is a larger thing going on here… It takes years of patterns to create the way we live. This program is designed to break patterns and habits so you can change your life without creating new habits. So the practices are consciously in order to increase four main points: **awareness**, **communication**, an **open heart** and **acceptance towards self**. *'Pathways to Love: 28 Days to Self Love'* is the foundation to feeling and expanding love in amazing ways, both inside and out.

At the end of each practice, there are journal pages to keep thoughts, doodles and awareness notes.

Each of the following pages will have the short practice, instructions and a set of icons. Here is a quick description of the icons, and how to use them.

The Suns

To help you stay organized, each practice will have this:

Each sun is a marker for a new day. You circle a sun to mark that you have done that practice once. There are 5 suns so that you can continue to use the marking system if you choose to do another 28 day cycle.

This is also helpful if you're sharing the book with another person like a lover or roommate. If two of you are following the book at the same time, just use a different-colored pen.

The Hearts

To help you rate the day's practice there is a 1 to 5 rating for each practice in the form of these hearts. There are two sets to help you if you want to continue a certain practice again later, retry something or if you are sharing the book. They look like this:

This is a quick way to create valuable feedback for your journey. If I was with you, I would ask you to share how a particular practice was for you. From there, we would know what we can work with, and what we need to work on. With this tool, you can do the same. Use whole and half hearts to rate your experience.

Glossary of practice symbols

There are other symbols that give you quick reference as to the activity and intention of the practice, and if there is a time consideration for it. You might find that you are fond of certain practice types. But remember, it's the ones you don't want to do that may offer you the greatest lessons.

Most practices are short and easy and don't require a lot of effort, yet there are others that you need to dedicate more effort to.

The glossary of practice symbols are:

 Meditation practice

 Consciousness practice

 Awareness practice

This tells how long the practice is (for a Timed Practice)

 Sensual practice

 Heart-opening practice

 Includes Music or Dancing

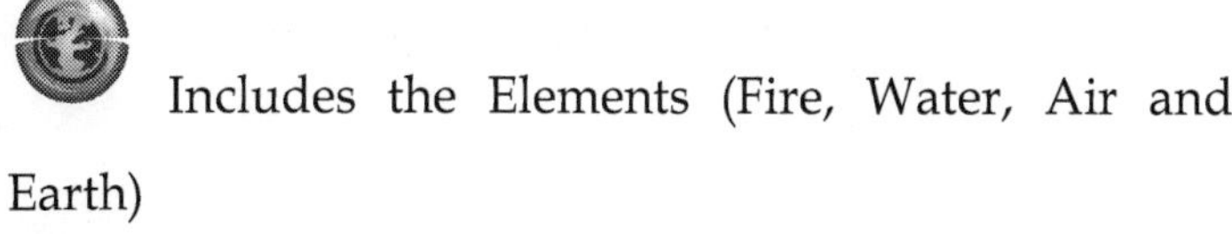
Includes the Elements (Fire, Water, Air and Earth)

Communication Skills

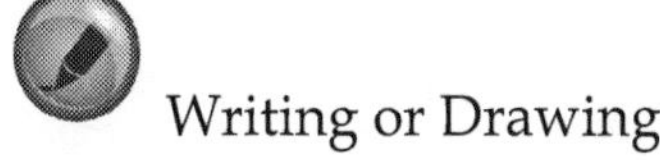
Writing or Drawing

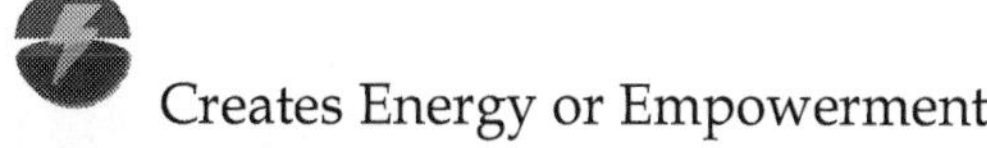
Creates Energy or Empowerment

Includes Food or Eating

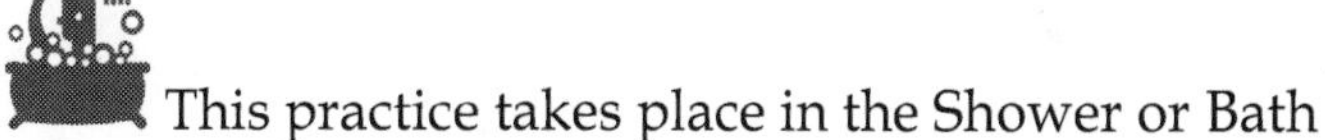
This practice takes place in the Shower or Bath

How to Start a 28 Day Journey

"What can we gain by sailing to the moon if we are not able to cross the abyss that separates us from ourselves?"

Thomas Merton

There are three simple ways to do this; each starts the night before so you can ready yourself for the next day's practice:

1. **The General Method**

   Do them in order. It's simple and structured. Just turn the pages each day.

2. **The Adventure Method**

   The night before you start, sit with the book, tune in and feel what's going on in your life. Now, open the book at random.

   If you picked a new practice in your 28 day

cycle, great! This is your next practice, have a go at it.

If you picked a practice that you've already completed, then:

a. If you opened and picked a left page, thumb back to the next undone practice.

b. If you opened and picked a right page, thumb forward to the next undone practice.

3. **The Freestyle Method**

   Find your own way through the next 28 days. You choose your own path of how you exercise the 28 practices. This is a more advanced recommendation.

   If you have completed the journey once or twice, this a great way to expand into the experience with greater awareness.

Use the method that works best for you.

It's Your Experience

This is your chance to soften the very thing that may keep you from loving fully. We all have past experiences that warrant our hearts to be shielded. The next 28 days will melt your guarded heart. You will see that every relationship you have been in is a mirror. There are lessons to understand in EVERY relationship. The most challenging thing for me in doing this work is hearing that the lesson learned was to love more cautiously and be more careful of whom you trust and share your heart with.

Ever so often, this is not the lesson at all! Many times the lesson is to remember to **love yourself first** and you will discover that being in a relationship does not need to be crazy or foolish as it has been in the past. Explore these 28 daily tasks as a chance to court with yourself again.

This is not about being alone… It's about remembering to keep your love healthy in all aspects of life.

Take your time, enjoy and write about what comes up for you. Be willing to share it with others.

This book is **not** about:

- Being alone
- Being single
- Hurting
- Blood, sweat and tears to get what you want
- Not having sexual relations
- Changing your faith
- Getting stuck
- Losing people

This book **is about:**

- Getting in touch with yourself
- Being aware
- Remembering to love
- Staying open to love

- Playing
- Enjoying a graceful life
- Being true to your core feelings
- Dropping the to need to react
- Letting go
- Forgiving yourself and others

Before you start, write your **intention** for the next 28 days. Not a goal, but more about what flavor you would like to experience with the program. *Intent* is more than just what one has in mind to do or bring about. *Intent* suggests clearer formulation or greater deliberateness. However, a *Goal* suggests something attained only by prolonged effort and hardship.

Webster's Dictionary offers this definition of

Intention[1]:

1: *a determination to act in a certain way; resolve*

2: *import, significance*

3: a) *what one intends to do or bring about* **b)** *the object for*

[1] www.merriam-webster.com

which a prayer, mass, or pious act is offered

4: *a process or manner of healing of incised wounds*

Be clear and on point, remember to stay away from an agenda or goals of what the end looks or should look like.

Your past experiences may be keeping you from the contemporary, fresh life you deserve to live. Release what you think you want, and allow yourself to express what you feel could support you in enjoying the next 28 days.

28-Day Intention for Self Love:

It's time to rise and fall in love with you again...

1.  10 minutes

Day Complete: 

Rate your experience: 

♡♡♡♡♡

Cut your cords from the past

*"The secret of health for both mind and body is not to mourn for the **past**, worry about the **future**, or anticipate troubles, but to live in the **present** moment wisely and earnestly."*

Buddha

There are ancient teachings supporting the idea that there are cords that connect people together.

Through these cords, things like emotions, projections, fantasies, needs and wants are shared. It's a process that energetically links us together. This is a chance to clear your cords and free yourself from that which might be holding you back. Many times the reason why we might get stuck in patterns is based on this very idea of cords and how we link with our relationships, thoughts and attachments. **Here is your chance to cut your cords and liberate yourself.**

This is an active meditation. Get comfortable and relax. See your heart open up and feel warm honey-like energy, start to rise up from your open heart. Let that energy fill your head as it starts to pour out the top of your head. Let that warm, honey like energy pour down your body, on the outside, creating a 2nd layer of skin. Just let the warm, thick, honey-like energy coat your entire body from the top of your head to the souls of your feet.

Let this heart energy cut any cords or past relationships. Let your heart's energy smooth out your body. Be slow and enjoy this cocoon of heart energy for 6-8 minutes. Feel your breath. Focus on your senses. You are releasing years of the past right now.

Then relax, take a deep breath in, closing the top of your head where this heart-river is flowing from. As you exhale, feel the 2nd layer of fluid skin drop into the earth.

Relax and enjoy a calm feeling for 2 to 4 more minutes.

Each time you cut your cords in this way, you release patterns and renew relationships by creating new energy exchange and letting go of old associations. You also cut free of any people, ideas or things that are no longer needed in your life, thus reclaiming your energy and vision.

It's OK to cut all your cords. Some of you might be very sensitive and attached to your connections. You will reconnect with the cords you need after the meditation. The awareness is to feel and notice the that don't serve your need to reconnect. Now use discernment to evaluate your connections. Maybe you didn't know some of the people whose energy is funky and no longer serving you, and how they corded into you. It's OK. Make a new choice. Support yourself and see patterns shift.

Dog ear this exercise; it is a tool that can be used anytime you feel out of center or in question.

Bonus Offer! Go to www.tantraquest.com and click on the Pathways to Love Tool Box to get audio this meditation guided by Shawn and other free tools and bonus practices FREE!! Log on today...

Cutting Your Cords Notes:

Share any insights or awareness.

Cords are my weakness & I hold on for way too long. It is time to let go to move on to my new life

2.    Morning Time

Day Complete: 

Rate your experience: ♡♡♡♡♡

Change the start of your day

"The only difference between a rut and a grave is their dimensions"

Ellen Glasgow

The mind loves routine activity. It seeks for a sense of control and order to things. The problem is that it also locks in certain emotions and patterns of how our day unfolds in a pattern, destroys the freedom of the heart to live in a wise, explorative way. Change your day, and patterns melt; thus offer your heart the chance to expand and experience the day in a new way.

Today you are going to shake things up a little, no major change is needed. Little adjustments create big transformation later, it just kind of sneaks up on you. The day to day patterns create a sense of comfort, but the nature of self love is to explore yourself outside the humdrum existence and embrace the true nature of you. Today is a new day. It's **fresh canvas.**

Look at what you normally do and the order in which you do it. Here is an example:

1) Wake-up
2) Bathroom
3) Coffee
4) Check email
5) Watch news
6) Eat
7) Shower
8) Dress

9) Off to work

Today, do as little in that order as possible and remove 2 things and replace it with something new.

1) Wake up
2) Bathroom and Shower
3) Tea
4) Dress
5) Take a light walk
6) Eat while out
7) Call mom
8) Off to work

See how fresh the day looks from the normal day to day activities?

We all have experiences of starting off the day differently and how it changes things. This will affect how your whole day goes. Remember the assemblies in school? How about the first day of a new School year? Field trips? Half days? These things broke the day-to-day cycles thus changing how we interact with the day as an adventure.

Be aware of how you feel and how you connect by shifting the normal pattern. Things may look new, people may relate to you differently, your locked-in cycle for the day may shift. This is good to open your heart and soul to an adventure.

Changing your Day Notes:

Share any insights or awareness.

3.

Day Complete: 

Rate your experience: ♡♡♡♡♡

Find one thing that authentically makes you smile today

"I find television very educational. Every time someone turns it on, I go in the other room and read a book."

Groucho Marx

This Practice is so easy, and if you are not aware, you could miss it. So peak your awareness today as to what makes you smile. Enjoy slowing down and move from reaction to conscious action. Lose the need to smile for the sake of it and reclaim a connection to what really allows you to glow as you smile.

- Notice how you feel.
- Watch how other people respond to you.
- How long does it last?
- Enjoy all that has made you smile.

Authentic smiling creates deep heart opening, and again, it's just so easy!

It's non-verbal communication. You know this, and have learned to use the smile to defuse situations, in conflict avoidance, emotional concealment, shyness, or embarrassment. This practice is amazing in having **SELF TRANSPARENCY**. Only you really know what your smile means and how it feels. Again, it seems like a simple little thing, but it has the opportunity to create massive awareness on how non-verbal communication connects to how we relate to ourselves.

Smiling Notes:

Share any insights or awareness.

4.

Day Complete: 

Rate your experience: ♡♡♡♡♡

Enjoy a meal alone today

"To be alone is to be different, to be different is to be alone."

Suzanne Gordon

There is a large amount of energy that can't flow until you learn to enjoy yourself, until you come back into that space of a healthy aloneness beyond all the social conditioning. This is where you are fine if you're with someone, or if you are by yourself. This is a hard place for some. Start with small, easy steps. This will lead to liberation; a change in how it feels to **spend time with you**. This freedom is your birthright.

So much is said about humans as social beings. I agree. However, many of us have given the outside world too much responsibility to measure us on whom we are. In research for this book, I came across dozens of studies linking aloneness to depression. I can't remember one example while growing up, where I was taught aloneness is a healthy act. So I grew up seeking people to meet that need, to fill a relationship emptiness…an emptiness that no one else can fill!

I never understood being alone as a healthy thing; In fact, I felt guilty being alone at times. Being alone is not the core issue of depression, as many may feel. Its acceptance that so many are seeking. So, finding out who you are and healthy ways to live that way affords you an opportunity to return to your true nature. This can release stuck depression and opens the heart to receive the gifts of self knowing without projections.

When you find times that you like spending time with yourself, it's amazingly graceful to share this with others. As with all relationships, we are learning to like and accept ourselves, which leads to love. That love becomes a magnet for others, because you are living from self love.

Take yourself out for a meal alone, by choice. Being alone is important. Eating alone can be a very introspective time for you. Turn off the phone. Maybe bring a journal or pad to write on or a book. Enjoy your company. It's a gift to make time for you. Be aware of your feeling or any old patterns of self judgment.

Look for the celebration of this meal. Feel the freedom that you had the choice of what, where and when to eat this meal. It's all about you, take it in and witness how it feels.

Bon Appetite!

Afterwards, write a journal about these things:

- 3 things (if any) that challenged you.
- 3 things you enjoyed.
- Did you learn something new about yourself?

Meal Alone Notes:

Share any insights or awareness.

     15 minutes

Day Complete: ☼ ☼ ☼ ☼ ☼

Rate your experience: ♡♡♡♡♡

♡♡♡♡♡

Write about a relationship from the past, focusing on the good

"Life's challenges are not supposed to paralyze you; they're supposed to help you discover who you are."

Bernice Johnson Reagon

One of the main barriers to an open heart is holding on to memories that hurt us or keep people from being seen in positive ways. Your past relationships are best to understand, learn from and get that they don't have to become the baggage you carry into your new relationships or your relationship to self.

Today's practice helps strengthen the connection to loving. When we get hurt, many times the focus is on the pain or displeasure that we are holding from the past. The people who we can feel so bad about are usually the people we also carried great love for. Can you see the neurological/emotional connections that are possible?

Spiritually speaking, the releasing of the past is like cleaning house. If you are attached to a bunch of stuff from your past, and you have little room to keep it, but you do keep it only for emotional reasons, it is causing attachment. Most people are focused on not being able to let go; but the trick is to embrace why you love it and understand it may not support you today like it did in the past. Then, the possibility for release becomes greater.

Emotional baggage is the same. Carrying anger, past love hopes, guilt, fear or pain may be taking up the space that could be open for new experiences and connections. This practice will help soften the heart by celebrating your loving ability.

Find 3 things that you remember from a past relationship that totally made you enjoy and love this person. Focus on that and remember the happiness and laughter you shared. Remember the little things that made you smile. Meditate afterwards and journal your feelings and any awareness. Focus on what worked out rather than the person. Stay with your open heart while being available to all kinds of feelings. If anger or sadness comes up, look at your list again and then stay in what works for you in love.

Notes:

Share any insights or awareness.

       30 min

Day Complete: 

Rate your experience: 

Enjoy some chocolate as a sensual experience

"... the taste of chocolate is a sensual pleasure in itself, existing in the same world as sex... For myself, I can enjoy the wicked pleasure of chocolate... entirely by myself. Furtiveness makes it better".

Dr. Ruth Westheimer

Oh chocolate; the divine food that sparks so much within us!

Ever since the first coca beans were gathered by the Mayans, there's been a knowing that chocolate has a elated impact on the body's senses. The conquistadores saw Emperor Montezuma of the Aztecs consuming a large amount of cocoa in a drink called *chocolatl* before going into his harem. The invading Spaniards spread the belief that cocoa was an aphrodisiac and brought it to Europe. It's also rumored that Casanova adopted this principle.

Since then, the use of chocolate as part of the mating ritual has continued. Modern research has shown that not only does chocolate increase the sexual appetite but also produces a sense of elation similar to an orgasm. Scientists have also unraveled chocolate's psychotropic properties and how it influences us. Chocolate contains modest amounts of the stimulants caffeine and theo-bromine. Chocolate also generates increased levels of serotonin, a chemical naturally produced by the brain, which is known to reduce anxiety. Serotonin is most commonly associated with the effects of marijuana or getting 'stoned' (but you would have to eat 25lbs of dark chocolate at once to achieve the same effect).

These properties on their own don't provide the connection between eating chocolates and heightened sexual pleasure. It's in the rush of endorphins produced by eating chocolates, mainly dark chocolates that is similar to bliss associated with a enjoyable sexual experience. Chocolate also contains phenyl-ethylamine which is known to stimulate the release of dopamine into the pleasure centers normally related with an orgasm.

Today, get some really good chocolate (I suggest a 70% cacao or more). Furthermore, have some fresh fruit to go with it like apples, grapes, berries, mango, peach or banana. MAKE SURE YOU WAIT TO EAT! NO NIBBLES. JUST WAIT.

Set up a relaxing space. Get naked. Have the chocolate on a plate and out of the wrapper. Arrange the fruit around the chocolate with some flowers maybe.

Start with a meditation of your mouth. Roll your tongue in your mouth. Just be aware. Now, open your eyes, take in your offering to you, but just gaze at it. This is foreplay; let your mouth become watery. Only when your mouth is well watered up, start the intake of the food, SLOWLY! Savor each bite. Experience everything going on in your mouth and body. Enjoy as you vary your bites of chocolate and fruit, and mix them. Don't expect anything, just witness. This can be very arousing, as you are making love to your taste buds.

Chocolate Notes:

Share any insights or awareness.

7.  All Day

Day Complete: 

Rate your experience: ♡♡♡♡♡

Smile more today and feel what your heart does

"Seeing a smile creates what is termed as a 'halo' effect, helping us to remember other happy events more vividly, feel more optimistic, more positive and more motivated."

Psychologist Dr. David Lewis

Smiling creates an invitation to connect in a heart space. Some people avoid smiling as a protection to keep such invitations away. Non-smiling has become a practice, it has created a long term association to that feeling of being "armored". This locks our movement of heart energy.

People who are **optimistic** (and these are the people who are out there smiling!) have stronger immune systems and are actually able to fight off illness better than pessimists.

"*The research is very clear,*" says Christopher Peterson, PhD, a University of Michigan professor who's been studying optimism's link to health for over two decades, "*This is not some social science generalization. There is a link between optimistic attitudes and good health. It has been measured in a variety of ways. Overall, we have found that optimistic people are healthier. Their biological makeup is different. They have a more robust immune system.*"

Further research shows that people who are optimistic are more likely to take care of themselves, which may be another reason why they tend to be healthier. Peterson continues, "*Optimistic people act differently ... [and] are more likely to do the things that public health experts say are associated with good health. Generally speaking, they eat sensibly, they don't drink senselessly, they exercise and they get their sleep.*"

Today, bring consciousness on how you share your smile. Let it be full, alive and welcoming. I'm not talking about faking it, but more about relaxing and surrendering to the smile response. The lack of smiling is a learned and controlled act. Let the smile spread across your whole being. Maybe it's a person, something you read, or think about.

This opens your heart, and soul, to share and experience more energy and vitality. It melts the armor. It can shift emotional states and patterns inside, as well as create opportunities to meet the day with a fresh approach.

Notes:

Share any insights or awareness.

8.    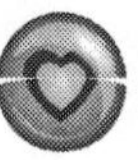  12 minutes

Day Complete: 

Rate your experience: 

♡♡♡♡♡

Light a candle and watch it dance for you

"Thousands of candles can be lit from a single candle, and the life of the candle will not be shortened. Happiness never decreases by being shared."

Buddha

Today, meditate with a candle. This is a yoga practice called *Trataka,* which is one of the six purification practices called *Kriyas,* and it acts as a stepping stone between physically orientated practices and mental practices, which lead to higher states of awareness. This is a great way to start feeling whole and connected to you. There are many wisdom schools that use this as a way to dance with your own inner flame.

Using a tea light candle or others, kiss the fresh wick with a flame, go slow and watch the flame transfer. Feel the warmth and change around you as you feel the flame embracing you. This act starts off as witnessing the flame and moves towards becoming the flame. Try focusing your eyes without blinking then soften your gaze and blur everything. Watch as your breath moves the flame and then, see if you can ask the flame to move for you. This is a courting of your inner power and example of your own soul flame.

Candle Meditation Notes:

Share any insights or awareness.

9.       

Day Complete: ☼ ☼ ☼ ☼ ☼

Rate your experience: ♡♡♡♡♡

♡♡♡♡♡

Shower Meditation: Feel your past being washed off

"Nothing in the world is more flexible and yielding than water. Yet when it attacks the firm and the strong, none can withstand it, because they have no way to change it. So the flexible overcome the adamant, the yielding overcome the forceful. Everyone knows this, but no one can do it."

Lao Tzu

I like to call the shower an *'urban waterfall'*. People love waterfalls in nature, and you have one in your own bathroom! Zen monks will stand under the falls, allowing hundreds of pounds of water to massage and pound them. This meditation is in part to remove that which is in the way.

Today, take a shower, as hot as you can handle. This shower is to clean not only your body, but your soul as well. Allow anything that keeps you from loving to be cleansed off.

Know that any perception of you being unlovable, undesired or unable to share love keeps the heart closed. Make a conscious choice to let the water clean that and close your eyes and bring the water element in as it supports a more flowing level of self-knowing and love. Let go of old concepts of who you are or what others think of you. Surrender and allow every drop of water to renew you.

Now, slowly, decrease the hot water, and get it as cold as you can, which creates a crisp, alive feeling.

Mint or Tea tree soap is great for this as well.

Shower Meditation Notes:

Share any insights or awareness.

10.   

Day Complete:

♡♡♡♡♡

Rate your experience:

♡♡♡♡♡

Listen to a song or album, and become aware of how it makes you feel

"I think music in itself is healing. It's an explosive expression of humanity. It's something we are all touched by. No matter what culture we're from, everyone loves music." **Billy Joel**

Music has energy to it. It affects us in amazing ways, and has deep unconscious connections to how we feel.

"Music changes our perception of space. Music can do all kinds of wonderful things for us. It's a wonder why most people don't realize that music helps them that much. Some people listen to music all day, all the time and they just think its music. It does something for them. That's what they say. But more people should fully understand that music might be the reason they haven't been sick in a year, or why they have such a low blood pressure for the way they eat." From the Campbell Index 73.

The music also goes deeply and creates beliefs and emotions. Favorite songs have a meaning, and many of them serve as a teacher or behavior creator through memories or associations—whether they serve your highest good or not. Many people love the song, "*My Heart Will Go On*" by Celine Dion.

OK, Wow! Do people really listen to these songs? It is anything but a love song, maybe a better wake song, but it is now associated with love, a very painful love at that.

Today, listen to a favorite song or album from your past. Enjoy those old friends with a new awareness. Really get into how your song(s) trigger things inside you. Many people hold time lines with music or have certain associations. Freshen up your emotional responses to these important songs. See how they live in you now. Understand you are new people everyday, and that you can release old anchors to the past.

Music Awareness Notes:

Share any insights or awareness.

11.

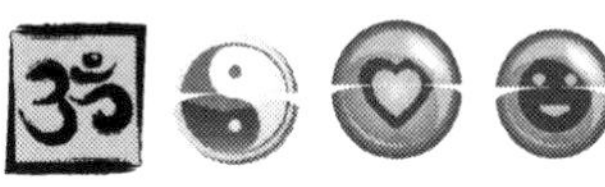

Day Complete: ☼ ☼ ☼ ☼ ☼

Rate your experience: ♡♡♡♡♡

♡♡♡♡♡

Strike up a conversation with someone who is helping you

"A single conversation across the table with a wise person is worth a month's study of books"

Chinese Proverbs

Meeting new people is the second biggest social fear (public speaking, of course, is number one), and yet everyday, there are so many people we come into connection with who help and support us, and make our lives easier. But rarely do we open up and learn more about these people. They might be the wait staff at a restaurant, the shopkeepers at stores, the mail person, or the security guard. They are part of your life. Opening yourself up can really offer amazing heart flow. The freedom that one feels in connecting without an agenda allows agenda-less connection in intimate situations. The fear of rejection is diminished, thus allowing us to learn human nature more. The key here is to know everyone is your mirror.

Today, say more than *'hello'* or *'thank you'* to one of these people. See how easy it is to learn about them. The gift in this is that you are allowing the veil to drop between you and others. This offers a great heart opening to who you are and how you feel about other people. Here are some tips:

- **Make eye contact**

  Let your eyes be soft and open, let your energy and feel come through them.

- **Smile**

  Be gentle and kind with your smile; create the invitation to talk more.

- **Comment about the situation**

  It's ok to open up and begin with something that you can both relate to.

- **Complement the other person**

  Again, it's a gift that can really change a person's day. Let it be small and real. (Wow, I really like your necklace!)

- **Ask a question**

These people are helping you, this is an easy opening to meet someone, it's like it gives you a reason to talk with them.

- **Ask for advice**

  This is an easy place to start a conversation; people love to give their own opinion.

Conversation Notes:

Share any insights or awareness.

12.

Rate your experience: ♡♡♡♡♡

Define what love means to you

"Love is being willing to accept all the failure and success one can bring. If I know someone I love can lie, hurt or abandon me, as well as please, play, enjoy and co-creation with me, the choice is easy. Love is too rich of an experience to control, hide from or deny. Knowing the whole range is

*what continues to offer me the freedom to love." **Shawn Roop***

Love is a code word…honestly. Many people don't think about the major components of what love means to them. Think about it. Love has so many meanings to everyone. Some people love it, others can't stand it. Love has many voices, aspects, desires and needs. What if everyone could share their concept of love? Maybe love would not be so messy if we could clear the assumptions, goals and definitions.

Here is what Webster's defines Love [2] as:

1a (1): *strong affection for another arising out of kinship or personal ties <maternal love for a child>* ***(2):*** *an attraction based on sexual desire: affection and tenderness felt by lovers* ***(3):*** *affection based on admiration, benevolence, or common interests <love for his old schoolmates>* ***b****: an assurance of love <give her my love>*

---

[2] www.merriam-webster.com

2: *warm attachment, enthusiasm, or devotion <love of the sea>*

Do you see how this may not fully express how you feel about love? Does it seem limited? Think about the power that comes with knowing what love means to you.

Today, take time to journal on your personal definition of love.

- What does it mean to you? Make sure it's a personal definition.
- Do you share it with others?
- Do you get this from others?
- Do you give this to yourself?

This practice may change how you experience love. It's a life question rarely understood and like sex, it's not shared openly, so there is a lot of room to make up things and impose projection. So many times while guiding people through this process, they share, *"It can be put into words."* I say *"Try,"* and I get a huge list of what love means. It's the work that creates masterful lovers.

What Your Code of Love Means:

Share any insights or awareness.

13.      7 minutes

Day Complete: ☼ ☼ ☼ ☼ ☼

Rate your experience: ♡♡♡♡♡

♡♡♡♡♡

Self pleasure with no agenda or goal

"We human beings are able to make love more frequently and

more sensuously than perhaps any other animal. Yet we are often disappointed after lovemaking. Why? Because most of us are like owners of a precious Stradivarius violin that we have never learned to play".

Jolan Chang

One of the most ancient, and overlooked, methods of centering yourself is careful cultivation of sexual energy. Wisdom systems like *Tantra* and *Taoism* create a wonderful connection to the deepest levels of sexual empowerment, and the use of self pleasuring is one of the most profound ways to tap into amazing meditative energy.

There are few times when people touch themselves sexually without an agenda. This creates a neurological association that when others touch us, there is an agenda. Change starts from within, so let's bring more awareness to this pleasurable act.

Today's practice is 7 minutes of touching yourself sexually with no agenda, fantasy or orgasmic goal.

This is to feel your skin, raise your energy, and enjoy the safety of being touched by a person who knows your body the best, you! Feel the trusting touch. You are your own best lover, and you always will be! Just 7 minutes today. Stay aware of how you feel. Are you annoyed? Are you frustrated? Are you bored? Are you energized? Are you turned on?

Use this to know yourself more.

This exercise is so important and offers you ways to open your heart while having sex. It can break the patterns and gives feedback of your sexual response and emotional connection to sex. If you go for the orgasm, you may miss this. If orgasm happens, cool, just don't seek it. Relax and enjoy!

Self Pleasure Notes:

Share any insights or awareness.

14.  30 minutes

Day Complete: ☼ ☼ ☼ ☼ ☼

Rate your experience: ♡♡♡♡♡

♡♡♡♡♡

Start to doodle as you think about love

*"**Self-love** seems so often unrequited."*

Anthony Powell

Maybe you've tried meditating and you've found that sitting quietly while paying attention to your breath isn't for you. Active meditation engages you in a mindless, repetitive activity that allows both your body and mind to relax.

Anna Koren, a foremost world expert in graphology shares, *"The process of doodling appears to only be a partially conscious one. Not once does it appear that the pen takes on a life of its own, and the "artist" himself is surprised by the results.*

One generally indulges in doodling while one's mind is on something else, rather than on the actual matter of doodling. People doodle in various situations - for instance, in the course of telephone conversations, lectures, while compiling lists and making notes".

You may have already doodled at some point, drawing squiggles and stars on the margins of notepaper while you're on the phone or sitting in meetings. Even if you aren't a natural doodler, you can learn to do this meditative doodle. The unconscious mind offers wonderful insight, if we let it. I always seem to smile when I get to see another person doodling while on the phone or something. There is just such a lovely stream of unconscious communication there.

Today, sit down with your journal. Be relaxed and turn off the phone. Use a pen you like. And start with the seed thought of love, and now start drawing whatever comes. Start with maybe 5 to 8 shapes, and let that guide you as a starting point. Keep doodling as you freely associate the thought of love. Don't try, just do. Let it flow. If you find yourself trying, stop, and start again in a new area on the same page. The idea is to fill the whole page to the edge without trying to fill the page, remember, this is a love meditation.

Allow this meditation to continue for 30 minutes.

Doodle about Love

15.

Day Complete: 

Rate your experience: 

♡♡♡♡♡

Enjoy a cup of tea. Focus on every aspect. Let it be a meditation of awareness

"If one has no tea in him, he is incapable of understanding truth and beauty."

Japanese Proverb

Drinking tea creates a distinct feeling of well being by itself and, when combined with a simple awareness meditation, it can reduce stress and prepares one for a stress free day and a life of health and longevity. The tea can be a single garden estate black, green, oolong or white variety, or one of the many quality blends on the market today.

You can start the meditation with the making of the tea or with the brewed tea already in front of you. Focus on the simple things; what cup or mug to use, the sound and smell of the kettle being filled. Hear the whistle and feel the heat from the tea pot. Be conscious of the brewing process, whether it's a lose tea or a tea bag.

Once brewed, let the cup's steam wash over your face and the smell penetrate deep. It's said the smell of tea caries deep wisdom from the past that many enlightened people smelled this same tea which supported their awakening. Notice the whole experience. Keep going deeper and reach inside as you approach this cup of tea as if it is the first cup of tea you ever had, and just descend into the sensations of that cup of tea so that the cosmos consists of only you, the cup of tea, and sitting.

The meditation is as long or as short as your body is comfortable with. You'll know a good session because your heartbeat will slow down, your breathing will deepen and you will feel refreshed but not hyper. This will support the rest of your day.

This simple exercise offers awareness to the simple things in life and allows you to feel connected in a more intimate way to the simpler, routine parts of the day. It's these very patterns that lock our magnificence in a box; only to be opened at "special" times.

Drink tea today, and connect outside the patterns and rewrite how amazing this life is. It's just a cup of tea...that could change your life.

Cup of Tea Notes:

Share any insights or awareness.

16.

Day Complete: 

Rate your experience: 

Buy, or even pick, flowers for yourself

"Bread feeds the body, indeed, but flowers feed also the soul."

The Koran

There is a happiness that we can get from flowers. There is an unconditional yet temporary love affair we can have with cut flowers. They offer sight, smell, and texture. There is such a connection to getting flowers as an act of romance and celebration.

You get to offer yourself this act today! Pick or gather your favorite flowers. Put them in a place that makes you feel special about the flowers, maybe in the bedroom or bathroom. Tend to them as they die. It's a whole heart experience from the happiness of the first sight to the sadness of their death.

We are like flowers. We are cut from our mother at birth and offered a chance to become independent. We will pass on. The key point is it's not the destination but rather the journey that counts.

Flower Notes:

Share any insights or awareness.

17.

30 minutes

Day Complete: ☼ ☼ ☼ ☼ ☼

Rate your experience: ♡♡♡♡♡

♡♡♡♡♡

Oil massage your feet, tickle your feet, and hold your feet

"Too often we underestimate the power of a touch, a smile, a kind word, a listening ear, an honest compliment, or the smallest act of caring, all of which have the potential to turn a life around."

Leo Buscaglia

Ah! The gift of a foot massage...how delicious! Every part of your body has a pressure point on your feet. Bring more blood to your body and increase sensitivity as you touch and activate healing by massaging your feet.

Dr. X. Ye of the Fudan University Medical Center shares, "*Reflexology or foot massage has long been part of Chinese tradition and culture. It is believed that foot massage cannot only maintain and promote health but also cure a variety of ailments. Foot massage is considered a form of relaxation and, to some extent, a luxury.*"

Today, love yourself by offering your feet a festival of sensual touch. Use an oil or cream you like. Put on some gentle music. Then sit down and begin to massage your whole foot. Be very attentive to the points that feel great. Allow yourself to really open up to the awareness of the touch.

Light touch and tickling is also encouraged to give the full range of sensation. Learning where you liked to be massaged is an amazing gift, it not only improves your own relationship to self but can also be shared with others.

Self Foot Massage Notes:

Share any insights or awareness.

18.

Day Complete: ☼ ☼ ☼ ☼ ☼

Rate your experience: ♡♡♡♡♡

♡♡♡♡♡

Learn *"I love you"* in three other languages

"Loving someone, and telling them often, is a gift. And not just to the recipient of your love, but to yourself as well."

Anonymous

The word love carries great energy and magic. It has been spoken by billions of people. When we use a word that carries such power, you can tap into the centuries of intention and energy.

Today, learn how 3 other cultures say *"I love you"*. Here is a list of 179 ways. As you say it in the new language, see how it feels. **Stretch yourself to learn three that you may never have heard before**. Who knows, the next time your making love, you might scream one of them!

Here is a list of 179 ways to say "I love you":

Afrikaans - *Ek is lief vir jou*

Albanian - *Te dua*

Alentejano (Portugal) - *Gosto de ti, porra!*

Alsacien (Elsass) - *Ich hoan dich gear*

Amharic (Aethio.) - *Afekrishalehou*

179 ways to say "I love you"...

Arabic - *Ana ahebak / Ana bahibak*

Armenian - *Yes kez shat em siroom*

Assamese - *Moi tomak bhal pau*

Assyr - *Az tha hijthmekem*

Bahasa Malayu (Malaysia) - *Saya cinta mu*

Bambara - *M'bi fe*

Bangla - *Ami tomakay bala basi*

Bangladeshi - *Ami tomake walobashi*

Basque - *Nere maitea*

Batak - *Holong rohangku di ho*

Bavarian - *Tui mog di*

Belarusian - *Ya tabe kahayu*

179 ways to say "I love you"...

Bengali - *Ami tomake bhalobashi*

Berber - *Lakh tirikh*

Bicol - *Namumutan ta ka*

Bisaya - *Nahigugma ako kanimo*

Bolivian Quechua - *Qanta munani*

Bosnian - *Ja te volim* (formally) or *Volim-te*

Bulgarian - *As te obicham*

Bulgarian - *Obicham te*

Burmese - *Chit pa de*

Cambodian (to the female) - *Bon saleng oun*

Cambodian (to the male) - *Oun saleng bon*

Canadian French - *Je t'adore* ("I love you")

179 ways to say "I love you"...

Canadian French - *Je t'aime* ("I like you")

Catalan (Mallorca) - *T'estim*

Cebuano - *Gihigugma ko ikaw*

Chamoru (or Chamorro) - *Hu guaiya hao*

Cherokee - *Tsi ge yu i*

Cheyenne - *Ne mohotatse*

Chichewa - *Ndimakukonda*

Chickasaw - *Chiholloli* (first 'i' is nasalized)

Chinese (Cantonese) - *Ngo oi ney a*

Chinese (Mandarin) - *Wuo ai nee*

Corsican - *Ti tengu cara* (to female)

Corsican - *Ti tengu caru* (to male)

179 ways to say "I love you"...

Creol - *Mi aime jou*

Croatian - *Volim te* (used in common speech)

Czech - *Miluji Te*

Danish - *Jeg elsker dig*

Dutch - *Ik hou van jou*

Dutch - *Jeg elsker dig*

Ecuador Quechua - *Canda munani*

English - *I love thee* (used only in Christian context)

English - *I love you*

Eskimo - *Nagligivaget*

Esperanto - *Mi amas vim*

Estonian - *Ma armastan sind / Mina armastan sind*

179 ways to say "I love you"...

Ethiopia - *Afekereshe alhu*

Faroese - *Eg elski teg*

Farsi - *Tora dost daram*

Filipino - *Mahal ka ta*

Finnish - *(Minä) Rakastan sinua*

Flemish (Ghent) - *'K'ou van ui*

French (formal) - *Je vous aime*

Friesian - *Ik hald fan dei*

Gaelic - *Tá mé i ngrá leat*

Galician - *Querote* (or) *Amote*

Georgian - *Miquar shen*

German - *Ich liebe dich*

179 ways to say "I love you"...

Ghanaian - *Me dor wo*

Greek - *Agapo se*

Greek - *S'agapo*

Greenlandic - *Asavakit*

Gronings - *Ik hol van die*

Gujarati - *Oo tane prem karu chu*

Hausa - *Ina sonki*

Hawaiian - *Aloha au ia`oe*

Hebrew - *Ani ohevet ota*

Hiligaynon - *Guina higugma ko ikaw*

Hindi - *Main tumsey pyaar karta hoon / Maine pyar kiya*

179 ways to say "I love you"...

Hmong - *Kuv hlub koj*

Hokkien - *Wa ai lu*

Hopi - *Nu' umi unangwa'ta*

Hungarian - *Szeretlek te'ged*

Icelandic - *Eg elska thig*

Ilocano - *Ay ayating ka*

Indi - *Mai tujhe pyaar kartha ho*

Indonesian - *Saya cinta padamu* ('*Saya*', commonly used)

Inuit - *Negligevapse*

Iranian - *Mahn doostaht doh-rahm*

Irish - *Taim i' ngra leat*

179 ways to say "I love you"...

Italian - *Ti amo/Ti voglio bene*

Japanese - *Anata wa, dai suki desu*

Javanese (formal) - *Klo tresno marang panjenengan*

Javanese (informal) - *Aku terno kowe*

Kannada - *Naanu ninna preetisuttene*

Kapampangan - *Kaluguran daka*

Kenya (Kalenjin) - *Achamin*

Kenya (Kiswahili) - *Ninakupenda*

Kikongo - *Mono ke zola nge (Mono ke' zola nge')*

Kiswahili - *Nakupenda*

Konkani - *Tu magel moga cho*

Korean - *Sa lang hae / Na no sa lan hei*

179 ways to say "I love you"...

Kurdish - *Khoshtm auyt*

Laos - *Chanrackkun*

Latin - *Te amo*

Latvian - *Es mîlu tevi*

Lebanese - *Bahibak*

Lingala - *Nalingi yo*

Lithuanian - *As myliu tave*

Lojban - *Mi do prami*

Luo - *Aheri*

Luxembourgeois - *Ech hun dech gäer*

Macedonian - *Jas te sakam*

Madrid lingo - *Me molas, tronca*

179 ways to say "I love you"...

Maiese - *Wa wa*

Malay - *Saya cintakan mu / Saya cinta mu*

Maltese - *Inhobbok hafna*

Marathi - *Me tula prem karto*

Mohawk - *Kanbhik*

Moroccan - *Ana moajaba bik*

Nahuatl - *Ni mits neki*

Navaho - *Ayor anosh'ni*

Ndebele - *Niyakutanda*

Nigeria (Hausa) - *Ina sonki*

Nigeria (Yoruba langauge) - *Mo fe ran re*

Norwegian - *Jeg elsker deg*

179 ways to say "I love you"...

Osetian - *Aez dae warzyn*

Pakistan (Urdu) - *May tum say pyar karta hun*

Pandacan - *Syota na kita!!*

Pangasinan - *Inaru taka*

Papiamento - *Mi ta stimabo*

Persian - *Tora doost darem*

Pig Latin - *I-yea ove-lea ou-yea*

Polish - *Kocham cie*

Portuguese (Brazilian) - *Eu te amo*

Punjabi - *Me tumse pyar ker ta hu'*

Quenya - *Tye-mela'ne*

Romanian - *Te ador* (stronger)

179 ways to say "I love you"...

Romanian - *Te iubesc*

Russian - *Ya tyebya lyublyu*

Samoan - *Ou te alofa outou*

Sanskrit - *Tvayi snihyaami*

Scottish Gaelic - *Tha gra\dh agam ort*

Serbo-Croatian - *Volim te*

Setswana - *Ke a go rata*

Shona - *Ndinokuda*

Sign language - *Spread hand out so no fingers are touching. Bring in middle & ring fingers and touch then to the palm of your hand.*

Sindhi - *Maa tokhe pyar kendo ahyan*

Singhalese - *Mama oyaata aadareyi*

179 ways to say "I love you"...

Slovenian - *ljubim te*

South Sotho - *Ke o rata*

Spanish - *Te quiero / Te amo / Yo amor*

Sri Lanka - *Mame adhare*

Surinam - *Mi lobi joe*

Swahili - *Naku penda*

Swedish - *Jag älskar dig*

Swiss-German - *Ch-ha di gärn*

Tagalog - *Mahal kita / Iniibig kita*

Tahitian - *Ua here au ia oe*

Taiwanese - *Wa ga ei li*

Tamil - *Naan unnai khadalikkeren*

179 ways to say "I love you"...

Telugu - *Nenu ninnu premisthunnanu*

Thailand - *Khao raak thoe / Chun raak ter*

Tunisian - *Ha eh bak*

Turkish - *Seni seviyorum*

Ukrainian - *Yalleh blutebeh / Ya tebe kohayu*

Urdu - *Mea tum se pyaar karta hu* (to a girl)

Urdu - *Mea tum se pyar karti hu* (to a boy)

Vietnamese (Females) - *Em yeu anh*

Vietnamese (Males) - *Anh yeu em*

Vlaams - *Ik hue van ye*

Vulcan - *Wani ra yana ro aisha*

Welsh - *Rwy'n dy garu di*

179 ways to say "I love you"...

Wolof - *Da ma la nope*

Yiddish - *Ich han dich lib*

Yoruba - *Mo ni fe*

Yucatec Maya - *'In k'aatech* (the love of lovers)

Yugoslavian - *Ya te volim*

Zambia (Chibemba) - *Nali ku temwa*

Zazi - *Ezhele hezdege*

Zimbabwe - *Ndinokuda*

Zulu - *Mina funani wena*

Bonus Offer! Go to www.tantraquest.com and click on the Pathways to Love Tool Box to get meditation guided by Shawn and other free tools and bonus practices FREE!!

19.

Day Complete:

Rate your experience: ♡♡♡♡♡

♡♡♡♡♡

Make your favorite meal today.

"Sex is like having dinner: sometimes you joke about the dishes, sometimes you take the meal seriously."

Woody Allen

We eat for many reasons. Food can carry an emotional response and memory. Food can support or break patterns. Comfort food is a great example of that. Spicy food has been shown to increase happiness and live food has been shown to support more energy. These are just a few examples.

Today, create your favorite meal. Make sure that the whole experience is part of the practice: the meal planning, shopping, cooking, eating and the clean-up. Each stage is a chance to do your own thing, without having to debate, advice or schedule. It's all about you. Enjoy the experience that you may have done many times, but today, add extra awareness.

If you feel like sharing this meal, invite someone you feel can share this experience with you fully. Let them know what you are doing, they will feel honored you are sharing it with them. But IT'S NOT ABOUT THEM, it's all about you. This is important.

Stay in the self love and, if you choose to share, share from the place of self love. This offers a place for others to know you better; it's very intimate to stay in your center and share from that place.

Favorite Meal Notes:

Share any insights or awareness.

20.

Day Complete: 

Rate your experience: 

♡♡♡♡♡

Call or email an old friend and share how much you enjoy them

"If a man does not make new acquaintances as he advances through life, he will soon find himself alone. A man should keep his friendships in constant repair."

Samuel Johnson

The act of gratitude supports self love. Allow yourself to open your heart to someone you care about. As much as we may think these wonderful thoughts, often the only time people hear or feel it is on holidays and birthdays. People are amazing everyday, you are amazing everyday. Open up, and cross the normal line of when to share with someone how you feel about them.

> *"Gratitude, when expressed, boosted that communal strength,"* according to a study's lead author, Nathaniel Lambert, a research associate at Florida State University in Tallahassee. The finding makes sense because, "*When you express gratitude to someone, you are focusing on the good things that person has done for you,*" he said. "*It makes you see them in a more positive light and helps you focus in on their good traits.*"
>
> Lambert and his research team tested the idea that expressing gratitude helps strengthen

> relationships in this way by doing three different studies.
>
> In one study group, 137 college students completed a survey regarding how often they expressed gratitude to a friend or partner. Results showed that gratitude was positively linked with the person's perception of this *'communal strength'.*
>
> *From www.empowher.com on 4/10/2010*

Make a special, loved one's day by letting them know how much you care for them. The more you share, the more you will feel the gift you are offering. Remember you are receiving as well as opening your heart. Notice how shy you might be, or how the other person receives it. It may be uncomfortable. Work past that because the end results are wonderful.

Contacting an Old Friend

Notes: Share any insights or awareness.

21.

Day Complete:

Rate your experience:

Dance naked at home today to a song you love

"All my joys are due to thee, as souls unbodied, bodies unclothed must be, to taste whole joys."

John Donne

Dance shakes up the body. It moves your blood. It allows you to say hello to your whole being. Certain music just seems to move us. The beat carries a relationship that gets us going. There are songs that just have this magic such as *'Twist and Shout'* by the Beatles. That song seems to just get people's butts moving, and keeps them smiling the whole time.

A ballroom owner and operator Karen Tebeau explains, "*A lot of times, when people come into the studio, it's because there's been a change in their life: a divorce or they've been through a period of depression. They (continue) coming in, and you see a big change. After a while, they're walking in with a sunny expression. You know it's the dancing that's doing that,*" she says.

But why dance when nude? There is innocence in our nudity. The modern society has created a shaming of your body being exposed. If you look at a child, they love to dance naked. It feels normal. This exercise is to reconnect your neurological pathways to your memory of zero body image issues. It's there. I have become very aware of the smiles that people have while seeing a child dance naked. We remember.

You have songs that make you move. Cue them up, close the blinds, crank up the sound, and get naked. Being naked is an act of freedom. You are going to dance free! Have fun! Who cares what you look like dancing naked when you are alone? Let it all go and just dance! Maybe you'll even dance to a few more after for extra credit.

SELF ACCEPTANCE is everything here. I'm not there to coach you and push you to make this happen. You have to feel yourself get comfortable with being silly, sexy or innocent. If you break your resistance, the reward is a deeper connection to loving yourself!

Dancing Naked Notes:

Share any insights or awareness.

22.     

Day Complete: 

Rate your experience: 

♡♡♡♡♡

Wake up early to watch the sunrise outside.

"Look to this day for it is life, the very life of life. In its brief course lie all the verities and realities of your existence: the bliss of growth, the glory of action, the splendor of beauty. For yesterday is but a dream and tomorrow is only a vision, but today well lived makes every yesterday a dream of happiness and every tomorrow a vision of hope."

Sanskrit Salutation of the Dawn

In India, the sunrise is a very spiritual time. Prayers and practice are offered to the new day. This is a time of rebirth and freshness. It's a new day to cleanse one's self of the past day's activities. It's also a time to enjoy the beauty of the new day and all that awaits us.

Wake up 20 minutes before the sunrise. Do nothing that you would normally do once you are awake; no coffee, shower, internet or eating, that kind of stuff.

Just get up, let yourself stretch as you feel the new day. Be quiet and slow. This is about being gentle and graceful. Ready yourself as much as you need to go outside. Find a place outside where you can be alone to watch the sunrise. Think of your heart's path and how you can love yourself more today. Let the breaking sunlight fill you.

Return to the day as normal. Notice how you feel throughout the day. Journal your experience.

Sunrise Notes:

Share any insights or awareness.

23.      10 minutes

Day Complete:

Rate your experience: ♡♡♡♡♡

♡♡♡♡♡

Meditate on the feeling of love

"Love yourself first and everything else falls into line. You really have to love yourself to get anything done in this world. "

Lucy Ball

Where does love come from? What is it that makes us feel love anyway? There is much research on this topic and the answers are not as simple as brain chemistry. The studies range form biological ties, to needing to bond, to love addiction.

Many researchers have speculated that we seek to fare in love with members of the opposite sex who remind us of our parents, you've heard that, right? Some even found that we might be predisposed to be fascinated to those who remind us of ourselves. In fact, cognitive psychologist David Perrett, at the University of St. Andrews in Scotland, did an experiment in which he morphed a digitized photo of the subject's own face into a face of the opposite sex. Then, he had the subject select from a series of photos which one he or she found most attractive. Dr. Perrett found his subjects always preferred the morphed version of their own face (and they didn't recognize it as their own!). Self Love realized in science…?

Love comes from many places. Let's explore how and where it shows up for you.

Close your eyes and relax. Watch what arises in you as you begin to meditate on the feeling of love. Breathe full and slow. Be mindful.

Where do you feel love in your body? How does it show up? Allow thought to rise and fall with ease. These are all clouds passing in your internal landscape. Attach to none of these thoughts; just witness them.

If you find yourself stuck, Pick a number between 8 and 15 and count backwards to 1, and then return to the focus of the feeling of love. Stay in this mediation for 10 minutes. Journal on any feeling or thought that feels important.

Meditation of the Feeling of Love Notes:

Share any insights or awareness.

24.      

Day Complete: 

Rate your experience: ♡♡♡♡♡

All day, be conscious of your touch

"Don't seek, don't search, don't ask, don't knock, don't demand - relax. If you relax, it comes. If you relax, it is there. If you relax, you start vibrating with it."

Osho

When you were growing in your mother, your arms and hands come from your heart. Your hand is an extension of your heart. The more you open your heart, the greater the energy you move with your touch. It's really amazing if you stop and think about how important conscious touch is. Remember a time in the past when you felt a touch reach right into you and warm your soul. We can do this, everyday!

Today, I am offering you a chance to be aware of the sense of touch. This is a deep Eastern practice:

"Sometimes we see a pleasant sight, sometimes we smell a pleasant perfume, sometimes we hear a pleasant sound, and sometimes we experience a pleasant taste or a pleasant sensation of touch. When we sit quietly, the memories of these pleasant sights, sounds, smell, taste, touch; flash in our minds. Even if we have not experienced a particular kind of pleasant sight /smell /sound /taste /touch, but have only read or heard about it, the imagination of these experiences still fills our minds." SN Goenka , Pg 135-137, Jaage Antarbodh (Hindi / Pali)-VRI.

Often, people touch without awareness. They touch because they are nervous, uncomfortable, or they have an agenda. Today, be mindful of your touch. Take notice when your hand reaches out to touch someone else or some object. See how much communication you can share with your touch if you are touching a person. If you are touching an object, what is your connection? Not all touch has to have movement; even still touch can be powerful. Really awaken to how your touch might be on autopilot, and bring consciousness to your hands and actions.

This begins the process of finding your integration between the conscious and unconscious minds. This is where you learn yourself, and see the interesting level of awareness you might have. Everything is good, enjoy your touch!

Touch Consciousness Notes:

Share any insights or awareness.

25.

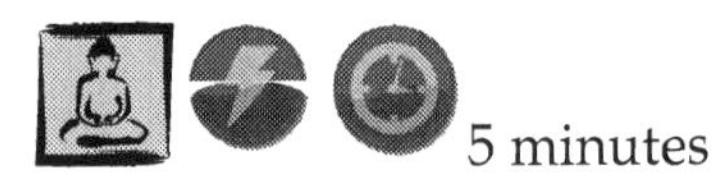 5 minutes

Day Complete: 

Rate your experience: 

♡♡♡♡♡

Rest with a cork in your mouth for 5 minutes to reduces stress

"Give your stress wings and let it fly away."

Terri Guillemets

The body doesn't know how to tell the difference between physical and psychological pressure. When you're stressed over things like: a busy schedule, a relationship, an argument with a friend, a traffic jam, or bills, your body reacts just as strongly as if you were facing a real life-or-death situation. If you deal with a lot of responsibilities and worries, your emergency stress response may be "on" most of the time. The more your body's stress system is activated, the easier it is to trigger and the harder it is to turn off.

Long term exposure to stress can lead to serious health problems. Continual stress disrupts nearly every aspect of your body. It can raise blood pressure, stifle the immune system, increase the threat of heart attack and stroke, contribute to infertility, and accelerate the aging process. Long term stress can even rewire the brain, leaving you more susceptible to anxiety and depression.

When people are under stress they often clench their

teeth. This can lead to tight jaw muscles. This tightness can spread to other muscles in the head and neck and may even contribute to back pain and tension headaches. The following stretching and massage exercise will help eliminate the problem at the source.

Open your mouth as wide as it can go so as to get a good stretch in the jaw muscles. Do this for a few times. Take your cork, and place it in your mouth vertical. Yes, the tips of the cork rest under your front and bottom teeth (and yes, it will fit).

Relax; let your jaw clamp down so that you do not need to try. Just relax. It may seem hard at first, but keep breathing and drop your shoulders. Maintain this pressure for at least thirty seconds at first. Relax without the cork for thirty seconds. Then repeat this cycle for four minutes straight. In time, you can increase the length of time you keep the cork in.

This will help train your jaw to stop clenching. Push on either side of your jaw until you feel a slight pain and massage the muscle a bit. This relaxes the tension that is there.

This will not stop your stress; it will reduce where we keep trigger point stress. Afterwards, you may find less need to react in stressful ways, and enjoy more centered and calm states.

Cork Meditation Notes:

Share any insights or awareness.

26.

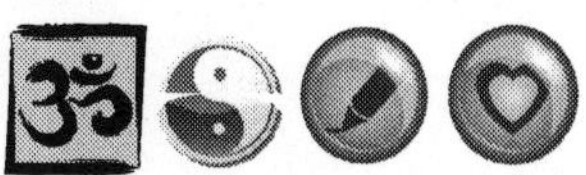

Day Complete: ☼ ☼ ☼ ☼ ☼

Rate your experience: ♡♡♡♡♡

♡♡♡♡♡

Forgive yourself for something in your past

"Finish each day and be done with it. You have done what you could. Some blunders and absurdities no doubt crept in; forget them as soon as you can. Tomorrow is a new day; you shall begin it well and serenely..."

Ralph Waldo Emerson

We all know the feeling of holding guilt about something and many of us struggle with the feeling of guilt all the time. Guilt can make us feel that we are somehow undeserving or unlovable. This issue really affects our overall well being each day. Feeling guilty is generally disempowerment from something in the past that cannot be changed. Guilt is a sticky emotion; it stays on, many times, far longer than needed. Rarely, are we motivated to forgive ourselves, make amends for mistakes, and move on; free yourself of the past. Guilt locks down the heart and gives reasons why one should not love. Yes, that's right; guilt can rob you of loving yourself.

You are going to offer your mind, body and spirit a great gift today. Become quiet and find an event in the past that you are still holding on to with the emotion of guilt. You are going to support the full awareness of all the elements of what happened to create this guilt.

Journal the lessons you received due to this event, and then offer yourself compassion and gratitude for your growth. This is a growth moment. Guilt is a simple emotion that is asking you to learn, so in extracting the lessons, release the held emotion of guilt.

Understand that you did the best you could in the moment, with the resources available to you. You are a human in the adventure called "life". Mistakes will be made. You will hurt people, you will let people down. That's what happens. Loving yourself means forgiving your short comings, while learning, so you can grow. **Acceptance** is the key to understanding love and allowing that love to expand and penetrate all areas of life.

Now that you have the learning in front of you, forgive yourself and release the chains around your heart. Small steps lead to great action, so for today; learn, forgive and grow. ♥

Forgiveness Notes:

Share any insights or awareness.

26. 

Day Complete: 

Rate your experience: 

Erotically map your body

"Map out your future - but do it in pencil. The road ahead is as long as you make it. Make it worth the trip."

Jon Bon Jovi

What a gift it is to have a lover know what they are doing. How to touch, kiss, tease and enjoy in the right places. When a person knows right where to go to evoke an energetic response, this may feel like they are a master. Have you had that? Are you still waiting to have that?

Wait no more! Today you are going to learn your body and you are going to map it out. This creates a masterful knowing of your own body. It's disempowering to wait for another to meet your needs. It can become co-dependant.

Start lighting some candles in your bedroom and putting on your favorite, relaxing music. Then take a hot bath or shower. There is blank page to take notes, so get a pen too.

You are going to go from the top of your head to your toes, mapping you body for pleasure. Tune in and really feel:

What feels good?

What feels just ok?

What is numb?

What areas surprised you?

What areas arouse you?

What tickled?

You will have your whole landscape mapped. Not only can you pleasure yourself there, but you can also share it with others!

The next page is for taking detailed notes about your mapping. Relax and have fun; honestly, the more you are into it, the more mastery you will get from it!

Notes:

Share any insights or awareness.

28.

Day Complete: ☼ ☼ ☼ ☼ ☼

Rate your experience: ♡♡♡♡♡ ♡♡♡♡♡

Write a poem about the sunset

"The heart feels oneness with existence while looking at a sunset, just for a second you forget your separateness. You are the sunset. That is the moment when you feel the beauty of it. But the moment you say that it is a beautiful sunset, you are no longer feeling it, you have come back to your separate, enclosed entity of the ego. Now the mind is speaking".

Osho

In the East, the sunset is a very magical time. It is said that during this time, all beings attain peace, tentatively ceasing from the tiresome monotony of worldly activities and take rest to resume creativity the next day.

Find a neat place to watch a sunset. Sit with your journal. Witness the day's end and open up your heart to whatever words come to you. Speak into feelings, thoughts and emotions. Create a small poem about this end of day and what it means to you. Add doodles or art. Let it be a creative lovemaking to the sunset.

Let the sunset burn your day. It is gone. Rejoice in the creation of the coming night, as you create a new day from nothing! This is the cycle, welcome in the moon.

Sunset Poem and Notes:

Share any insights or awareness.

The End?

The End of this book is not your goal; it's in the Now that you will find all that you seek.

There is a lifetime of love to create. Make love. Let it fill you, from you. Self Love is the secret of the masters and you took that path.

"Love is the outreach of self toward completion."

Ralph W. Sockman

'Enso' is the Japanese word meaning *'Circle'* which is used in *Zen*. **There is no end, no beginning. There**

just is. Your relationship to you is an ever unfolding occurrence. These experiences offered over the past 28 days are to remind you of the gift this life is and how rich it is to be you. The more you understand what an amazing part of this world you are, the more you will know love and how to share it.

You have arrived, and this journey is not over…

Ok, now what?

Congratulations to you! I celebrate your willingness to learn and explore yourself more through these practices. It's common that these simple exercises open the door to much more. That's my hope; that you got to pop on your pith helmet and really took on this adventure to open yourself up to more.

You may have enjoyed certain days more than others, and there are many factors to that; stress, emotion, business, health and so on. Relax from the need to judge your experience as good or bad. Each day is its own gem. Even if you hated a certain practice, there is wisdom you learned.

Again, this is about breaking old ways of how you were doing things. I could have given you the task to do each one a certain amount of times. That would have just created new habits or patterns. I support your empowerment and the release of doing things over and over. I want you to live life free and liberated.

Each day should be fresh and new, an empty canvas for you to create your amazing life.

This was all about opening your heart, increasing awareness and consciousness. All the mediations were active, to support your modern mind and its movement. We are busy people and loving ourselves can be very low priority on the list. This should change! Your relationship with yourself is the filter for all the relationships you have.

You just took 28 practices to task. Now it's time to mine a bit more. In your journal, take time to explore these questions:

- What did I learn?
- Which practices will I continue?
- Where am I holding back in love?
- What am I waiting for?
- Is there a fear in letting myself be seen in the world?

- Am I ready to love myself more than anyone, so I can share love from a pure place, without agenda?
- What do I want next?

Notes on your 28 Day Journey:

Share any insights or awareness.

Notes

Notes

There are many ways to get more from this point on.

But first, again, stop and celebrate what you have done. If you move on without this step, you will only be a *seeker of self love* rather than *one who is in self love.* You did it, not me. You put in the effort. That is amazing!

After a week or two, you can start the cycle again. Try it in a different way. Get a whole new journal to hold your writings. Do it all over again with a fresh outlook. Execute each day with an innovative approach. You most likely will get a whole new experience.

Many who take this journey start to awaken parts of themselves; sexually, spiritually, emotionally or energetically. This is a wonderful thing. Each breath offers us change and growth.

If you feel this has happened, I want you to know it was my intention for you to have whatever comes up, come up. It is all part of the new relationship to self.

Continue to learn more about you as these things unfold. Be willing to keep your eyes, hands and heart open. This is where that magic comes from each day.

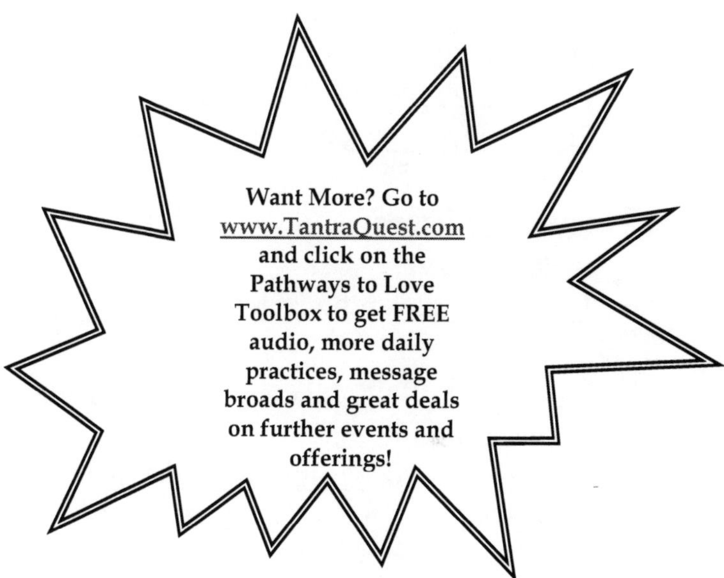

List of Practices

Next Books from Shawn Roop:

This is the first part in a three-part series of books on the **Pathways to Love**. The next title is:

'Pathways to Love: Adventures in Relationship'

This next book is all about practices and tools that will support you sharing love with others. I will explore communication, emotions, sex and co-creation, all the while staying centered and passionate. This draws off the rewards from doing the *'28 Days to Self Love'*.

The third book is

'Pathways to Love: In Quest of Spirit'

In this volume, I help you explore the relationship to spirit and the divine. This can be one of the most confusing love relationships to be in, yet it offers massive rewards. The book is full of ways to create a unique, full and tangible relationship to spirit.

If you want to go further, come to my workshops and events. These will help solidify the experience on a whole new level.

There will be more books and programs coming in the future to support you in exploring love, relationship and life. I will continue to help you in finding a path to a life well lived!

Coming Soon! 'Pathways of Love' **seminars and retreats**.

Work with Shawn in Person:

I also offer: **private counseling**, over the phone or in person, and would love to support you more right now if you are ready to go deep and get to your core issues fast, easy and now!

I can co-create a magical 3, 5, or 8 day retreat, just for you as well! This might be the most life changing experience has have ever had. Mention this book and get 10% an private retreats starting at only $799!

I am always creating and giving classes and workshops on *Tantra,* energetic psychology, relationships and life wisdom, all over the world. You can find out more about my work at:

www.TantraQuest.com

www.ShawnRoop.com

Send Shawn your comments and questions to this email:

Shawn@TantraQuest.com

If you are willing to share your experience of your 28 days to self love, we would love to hear from you. Times are changing and many are seeking more from life. Look for support groups, new programs, seminars and books coming soon to create a Life Well Lived in all areas of your world!

Shawn Roop is available to speak at your events or workshops. Shawn is also available for media appearances and projects. He also loves to co-create on ventures and other visionary opportunities.

Books are available in bulk at a discount from Jai Media.

Contact Jai Media at

619-481-8036

A teacher of mine once said...

"Learning to love oneself is not difficult, it is natural. If you have been able to do something which is unnatural, if you have learned how to love others without loving yourself, then the other thing is very simple. You have done the almost impossible. It is only a question of understanding, a simple understanding, that "I am to love myself; otherwise I will miss the meaning of life. I will never grow up, I will simply grow old. I will not have any individuality. I will not be truly human, dignified, integrated."

And moreover, if you cannot love yourself, you cannot love anybody else in the world."

Osho

Loving yourself opens the endless possibility to love others. Enjoy being your own soul mate and love full on! Remember, this choice is offered every day. Be kind to yourself and give the grace of love abundantly on all levels inside and watch your life expand.

I wish you much love and celebrate the life adventure that waits in each breath!

Shawn

Made in the USA
Lexington, KY
07 June 2010